PART OF THE BARGAIN

PART OF THE BARGAIN

SCOTT HIGHTOWER

 COPPER CANYON PRESS

Cover art: *Untitled (Cowboy)*, 1999, by Richard Prince. Ektacolor photograph, 61" x 32½". Courtesy of Barbara Gladstone Gallery.

Copper Canyon Press is in residence at Fort Worden State Park in Port Townsend, Washington, under the auspices of Centrum Foundation. Centrum is a gathering place for artists and creative thinkers from around the world, students of all ages and backgrounds, and audiences seeking extraordinary cultural enrichment.

LIBRARY OF CONGRESS CATALOGING-IN-PUBLICATION DATA
Hightower, Scott.
    Part of the bargain / Scott Hightower.
        p. cm.
    "2004 Hayden Carruth Award."
    ISBN 1-55659-232-9 (pbk. : alk. paper)
        I. Title.

PS3608.I37P37 2005
811 .'6—DC22

98765432
FIRST PRINTING

COPPER CANYON PRESS
Post Office Box 271
Port Townsend, Washington 98368
www.coppercanyonpress.org

Grateful acknowledgments to the editors of the following publications, in which these poems—sometimes in earlier versions—first appeared:

&. Journal for the Arts: "*Interior with an Egyptian Curtain*"

Barrow Street: "Falling Man," "Edge of the Knife", "Filicide"

Blue Mesa Review: "At the Trough"

Columbia: A Journal of Literature and Art: "Indian Summers"

Gulf Coast: "Blue Seville"

James White Review: "Portrait of Hartley"

The Journal: "Rose Hill"

The Paris Review: "Spending the Night," "Dildo Lob," "Scandal Fatigue"

Salmagundi: "Dinner of Grief"

Western Humanities Review: "Charles Laughton," "Practice Fitting: Marie Ponsot"

To my mother

CONTENTS

Behold how in the evening sunset-glow
The green-encircled hamlets glitter.

Goethe, *Faust*

DOOR TO THE TERRACE

— an invocation to the muse

I have a preference for peaceful nights
When I am alone; however, you are
Just as likely to show up mid-morning
Or late afternoon, past the glass door

Of the terrace. Losses and brutalities
Have left me dull. (I am as equally
Likely to be visited by the dead
As by the trials of the wandering living.)

Bubbling lagoon, black feather, sensuous
Viper, eyes of something greater:
Impulses slip into the structure.
Your voice is always voluptuous.

You withdraw from me like a match
From a final cigarette and dance every
Abandonment. The strains of music
That accompany you float away with you.

POLIO AND COUNTING

My brother, sister, and I
Were often taken to the fields
And sat on a patchwork quilt

In the shadow of a tree.
Each round our father made,
He would eye us in the shade.

Sometimes he would
Come down to move us
Or take a swig of water

From the burlap-wrapped
Can he'd stashed with us.
Our nanny was an English collie.

By four, I could reliably
Count sheep in multiples,
A skill honed sitting

On my mother's legs —
Her reclining on a raked
Sit-up board *her* father

Had gerry-rigged. Every
Morning she cried brushing
Her hair. The pain was simple.

Her perfume bottles glimmered:
"There will be pains that will not
Leave you with a kiss."

"AIDA"

To the limit: jotted score, script on paper,
shadows floating on a translucent scrim,
translated lyrics displayed or projected
on a screen. Cleopatra, Mata Hari, Antony,
your time is up (beyond the pomp, curse,
and reprisals). Here is your fatal scene. . .

*

In 1967 in the beautiful capital city
of Cairo, much of an ancient public park
near the Opera House was destroyed
when beloved trees were uprooted
to construct a modern bus terminal.

DIPPING INTO THE KITTY
When it succumbed to flames in 1972,
some thought corrupt officials
had deliberately set fire
to the illustrious center
to cover up their theft
of expensive costumes.

*

There are no other friendlier beckoning
lands, Gorges of Napata! Now only
Amneris in seclusion on the mezzanine
behind a mashrabiya screen
(boundless waste for a bridal bed)
prays, sobs, drinks in
what drifts in the littoral breeze.

"Sciava, Fate may have been
your guide, but you are
now only in Love's hands—
everything risked for Love." Ciao.
To be swept away hopelessly
in love; beyond the bed, beyond
the bend, Gebel Barkal, source
of the pharaoh's uncurtained fire.

Conundrum, great binding
secret! To be swept away
beyond the ineffable pageantry,
Kabuki, Kathakali, opera.

Two slight flames
burn in the blackness.

LETTING GO

Once, I was a swinger; not of birches,
but of swings. I liked the pump
and then the exhilaration of letting go.

Sometimes my own wastebasket runs over,
a bounty of faux postures: "imp's work,"
the stink and dangle of the swarthy impostor's
seductive sequence of smokes. No, not the slow
hoist and shift of matrimonial satisfaction
but the quick burn of a low grade: a shill
to mask the stench in the ditch.

The genuine thing wears a dab of patchouli
or a dab of rose water — or peonies —
and never vamps; only smokes
after words, and, even then, it is just
a couple of puffs on a clove cigarette.

"First — Chill — then Stupor — then the. . ."

I lean; but not so much toward the residual
insistencies of paralysis. Perhaps
from the experience of witnessing
my mother navigate herself
through the legacies of polio,
I catch myself leaning more toward
gleaning the authenticity and enduring
glimmer of proportion and perspectives.

AFTER POLIO

washboard muscles
were an impossibility.

Mother sat at a mangle,
controlled the pedals with her knees;
navigated the wrinkled
pillowcases and blue jeans
with her free hands. Sprinkled
and bagged the laundry one afternoon,
stored its balance in the refrigerator
till she could get it out the next.

Each afternoon, she read
to the three of us
while we nestled like piglets
at her belly and fantasized

oblivious of the evil
that had blown
against our front door.

AT THE TROUGH

. . . something unspoken, then . . .
J.D. McClatchy, "My Sideshow"

I'd gone from rinsing
toys with the hose
to fencing with my father

and his men. One afternoon,
preparing to wash off
the day's grime at the trough,

I began to undress
beside the sun-warmed
water. A lingering hand,

who had worked that day
alone, came in. A line
of wire had snapped:

the vicious recoil
of its teeth had sliced
his pants and gashed him.

I squatted and tried my best
to stanch and clean
his wounds. In the end,

the nearly exhausted man
brushed aside the conventional
goodbye-grip. Instead, he grazed

me with a kiss. That night, I
washed alone; for the first time
turning an undisclosed tension.

9

SPENDING THE NIGHT

Now, in another part of the country,
I hear it called "staying over."
Back then, a couple of years
was a gaping difference.
The ornately carved door
covering the strings of an upright
melded into the headboard
of the bed. He asked
if I had found my way yet
to lending my hand to another guy.
At first, it wasn't clear to me
what he was asking for.
I was barely in my teens,
naive and proud. He
was breathtaking,
stretched out in the dark,
at ease in his white cotton briefs;
his elbows extending out, his fingers
interlacing behind his head;
confident, handsome,
and merciful. And, though he
never pressed his lips to my lips,
he did not find any need
to rebuff my clumsy fingers.

UNDEPENDABLE

for R.G.

Montjoy is standing not far away —
Just behind our waiter, taking my measure.
I can feel the ears of Proculeius, Dolabella,
And Enobarbus fishing up at me
From the olive of my martini —
A dry, salty fish dangling off my hook.

Your tale, a response to your grandfather's
Words: where there should have been a poem,
His malicious lips betraying his own shallow,
Prosaic nature. Pertaining to you: green,
Orphaned, and emotionally nearly broken,
"Si es tan débil, aplástale la cabeza
Con una piedra." The merciful doctors blanching
At the ground of his flinty sympathy.

*

My tale of looking into the eyes of a migrant
Worker and reaching erotically through
The jargon; bootstrapping through to something
Like, "Traigo carne. Como están todos?
Trabajan mucho y mi padre está contento con . . ."
". . . la cerca." He completes the sentence for me.

"Sí . . . la cerca." I am not dependable.
I exercise my privilege to not portray
My father. The entitlement of his tonal
Cruelty, cultural condescension, and malice
Fails to dangle off my unexacting tongue.

*

Oh, wanderer, nights of uncertainty,
Let your rapture come to rest
In a city of fantastic prosperity:
Even Dido, under a beautiful African sky,

Tried to check her pathetic rage
On a pillow: "I should have calmly
Served up his son to him in a hideous
Feast." Instead, there was a single arrow

Dropped among the cushions. Someone
Else's heart going unpierced. Instead,
There will be a pyre of wasted gifts;
A wounded heart decorous in angry flames.

DILDO LOB

From the ten-year-old's conversation stopper
deployed to shock, "dildo" (and astoundingly
sophisticated in its rhetorically having been
tucked into a question, as in, "Do you have one?"),
to the adults' disarray and clumsy old bait-
and-switch tactic — their unfamiliar lips
closing ranks.
   "*Discretion,...*"

(A carefully aimed sortie counters
across the fajitas and margaritas.
The fastidious politeness of the syllables
cruises glinting and sharp. The blade
of the restaurant ceiling fan churns the air.)

"... another word for a dictionary foray"
(*Spoil* or *Pillage*). The adults
at the table yoke in their recovery;
their strength rising from ample
familiarity with Irony, Deceit, Malice.

There had been the stunned mother:
the silence and fading secrets
of generations of young rural women
descending; parents with daughters
worrying; and all the shame of an Eve.

There had been the pause, the dent
made by a word shot from the hip;
the concealed wrench of a napkin.
Shameless attention grabber:
the easy bravura of urbane crude
like granules of sugar on a boy's lip.

SCANDAL FATIGUE

Your rare "Dulcinea" arrives being brandished
over the heads of other denizens. Minutes
later across our plates, you start to ask
if the wallet you gave me a few weeks earlier
is being stuffed with money. But mid-sentence...
you rephrase your question. (You know
I dislike slang like "dead presidents.")

Who said, "The opposite of Luxury isn't Poverty,
but Vulgarity?" We mistakenly settle on Wilde
and agree we're fed up with the media constantly
excerpting and then looping salacious details,
with celebrities garnering dubious windfalls,
and with the disingenuous racket of broadcast
celebrities: babble lying down with the hydra
of talking heads. But, considering one
president's infantile lusts or another's covert
greed, neither is the first embarrassment
of low crimes in high office. Hard to tell,
exactly whose privacy is at stake?
Who's cheated? Who pays? Some
commentators chew on "abuse" but few
cut to the real, amazingly unsubtle, heart
of the matter — the banality of power. Few
of their clucking tongues ever venture toward —
much less attempt to commandeer — *honor:*
the factor that equates one's divvy of the spoils.

CONJURING WAR

Imagine (if possible) a woman dressed in an endless
garment, one that is woven of everything the magazine
of Fashion says, for this garment...

Roland Barthes, *The Fashion System*

Beyond rough magic, failure of the social
imagination, and freedom charmed
by vigor uneven; the military solution
raptures slavery, class, and prostitution:

sole resort to systematic
haunting, human will to will,
the privilege of hunting,
and the pose of liquidating doubt

(access driving out sacrifice,
feast, excess and its trembling):

status, possession,
and material advantage;

an eye trapped in a perspective
from an artificial green,
a turquoise pool; a tongue
curling in a reservoir. Perhaps
once it was a baroque carriage,
a grotto, a dance step,
or an ammunition sleigh.

Now, in power grids
of stuctural paradigms
and conflations of language,
is there any right or left left;

15

or just a vertigo, a trajectory
of devalorized seductions,
a wicked glow of abstract
pleasure and — faux pas —
real humiliation and torture?

Rather than reveling in
ghostly metaphors,
we are better off rapt
in a sacred plume of praise.

GOODS

in memoriam José Olivio Jiménez
December 5, 2003

This time, the lament
is not a bounce off water pouring

from the Fountain of Conches.
Nor is it composed

of a painted fan
evaporating on a breeze

not far from a Spanish sky
or a swirling American sea.

Another time, another place.
Once, in an Austin evening,

stirred by my own poor translations
of Cernuda's serenades,

the pounding hooves of the heroic
horses of Littlefield Fountain

tried to spell out for me
one just principle.

Man is a wing. Love
is the sun that melts everything.

You already had gotten the news
from Martí: *Aquellos cuyos actos*

son guiados por amor,
viven eternamente.

*El amor es el vínculo
entre los hombres,*

*el método de enseñanza,
y el centro del mundo.*

FALLING MAN

Sink then! Or I could also say: arise!
Goethe, *Faust II*

Forget about the burning towers.
The verticality of the valley
between the two of them.
Who hasn't been hurled into existence?

There are people in boats
in a distance on blue water.
And birds float through blue air.

The falling man floats,
too, artfully cartwheels
like a parachutist spiraling
into the slipstream's inner depth.
This is a threshold. It is spring.

A firm stance in the world
is illusive. "Condemned
to earth — with all
its terrors and beauties —
and to live there,
ejected from the dream-ship
in which the angels
continue on their way."

VIRGIL AND CAESAR

*There is neither Jew nor Greek, there is neither
slave nor free, there is neither male nor female...*
Galatians 3:28

Military patronage builds roads;
distributes honor, salt, money,
tracts of appropriated land,
justice, and citizenship.
Perhaps not such an odd alliance:
a metropolitan autocrat
(a designing patron
with a dream) and a poet
mindful of entailments
and resentments.

      *

*I can't quite put my finger on it;
his voice—at times, almost reconciling
with the fire—is familiar in its conviction.
Lit with a little wine and original authority,
his vision manages to stay on course
like a good soldier's pace on gravel.*

      *

A scribbler notes someone plowing in a field
and turning up an ancient sword,
evidence of someone's
sad defense
of appropriation.

*

"Even after Caesar,
the Galatians of Turkey
will speak their Celtic tongue."

*

If I build again the things that I
destroyed, I make myself a transgressor.

*

So many wills attached to a prize
worth saving. Unlike Aeneas
who had no choice in any of his trials.

ENVY-IN-LAW

yet at the first
I saw the treasons planted.
Shakespeare,
Antony and Cleopatra, I.iii.25–26

I've come expecting a domestic blue sky,
an almost convent calm, and the serene
perfection archaic paintings, songs,
and vintage postcards allude to:
perfect weather for reviewing the legends
carved in the speckled granite
tombstones of my connections
". . . established and maintained
the tone of a family-centered life,"
". . . a keeper of animals."

This is where I learned there can
be harshness without malice.
My mother, down on her knees,
is containing her hands in the beds,
a seething queen raking through ruined
finery. She paws at a weed.
"We'll not have any
in *this* family. That's *not*
how *you* kids were raised!"

Her forehead and neck glisten with sweat.
Branches shadow. No gloves or basket.
Her voice is an aphorism. I recognize
First Corinthians. Mother tiger.
Love-of-the-bride be damned.
No green-eyed monster
will be tolerated in this hen's house.

WHISPER CAMPAIGN

someone who resents
that their key is not sovereign
has an interest in keeping
everyone else from the lock,
shameful pilot and channel,
tongue like a knife,

whether it's for silver
or for delight in shade,
what gets designed
is a hungry goat traveling
outside the joy of camp,

not so much the nadir's "submission,"
the Pharisee's gleaming parade
of "obedience to the law,"
the missionary's "love in action"

as the skulking assassin
in the corrosive shadow
of pomp and malice,
disdain of enigma,
cartel, stealthful bomber,
worm in the night

STANDING GUARD

the coiling spell
of protection
from armless valences
blooming in the dark,
the jungle, the desert

Burmese fraternal order —
unhooded, skilled; shield
of initiation and dexterity:
snake emergency 9-1-1

ink: emulsive script: carbon,
ground black-peppercorn fine,
suspended with cobra
and Russell's viper venom,
injected, and lodged:

suspended black fire dotting
some verge of scalp: oaring,
the line of literal amulet
plowed in a chest
or at the base
of a vulnerable spine

*

the porous and shapely
Andalusian water jar,
(its small square tray beneath it
to catch any perspiration,
any single random drop)

the meandering script around it:
like a steadfast dog;
lyric and harp; lucky
locket, cameo or intaglio;
corral of cactus;
larder; wardrobe;

    *

trellis, rose, and thorn

WILD STAB

oh, not the clean incision
of an experienced surgeon,
the saber dragging a deliberate
legacy in the sand, messiah
come as a sword to divide good
from evil: the graced from

(as my grandmother
referred to them)
the Great Unwashed;
this week's supply
of mutton from the next
flawless holiday lamb;

nor the puncture of love,
thorn of life, the tip of
its septic spine withdrawing,
the wound, warm and wet
(almost clean), closing
but leaving a soft spot

rather than the penultimate
agenda, gist, veneer, japan,
lacquer of the soul; this is
the raw, the seat of one's pants,
payday, the unlearned,
unmitigated drive

BEYOND RANSOM

July 16, 1918

KOPTYAKI: Drums of gasoline;
measured volumes of sulfuric
acid; axes and saws;
handy site of an abandoned
pit in a remote mine shaft.
At the peasants' "Four Brothers"
(once haunt of four lonely pines),
mute sentinel stumps,
the sloppiness of goons
already has stirred the mud.

EKATERINBURG: Twelve
military revolvers. Past are
the mauve and cream rooms
filled with hyacinths, violets,
and lilies of the valley.

A burst of bullets
glints off holstered
gems — random sparks.
Smoke roping: everything
belief and disbelief.
A rustle of protection?
... "Divine intervention?
His will, *her* shield?"
The deepest of fears
blink and stammer
and everywhere
the swallowing reports.
With each acrid
trigger finger

pointing into
an abyss, the old
contest shivers.

Precious stones sewn into cuffs
and heart-armor corsets
betray the Czarina's secret.
Misguided clasp of inborn love

like a spaniel, a sapphire in a stay,
or one of the cracked rubies
strewn alongside the pierced
and bludgeoned bodies;

tendons, muscle, bone
transported, hacked,
sawed, doused — lit,
raked, and dumped;

valet, cook, parlor
maid, and doctor;

husband, son, daughters;
arm, jaw, and finger;

the once claimed legacies
and sparkling accessories
of service and sweeping
privilege ground into grass.

THE AUTOBIOGRAPHY OF ETHEL WATERS

When I was young, I took the changes
of nest and hive for granted

until I went through a spell
where nothing was enough.

I joined a book club at school, ordered
books, and—when we ventured

to the city—sifted through paperbacks.
Somewhere in Austin the autobiography

of Ethel Waters cost me fifteen cents.
How could I have known

what was in store for me
given the comfort

of *His Eye Is on the Sparrow*
in gold across a field of blue cotton?

Stung, I never remembered having
read anything quite like it:

that a stranger could hold
a knife to a young girl's throat.

Then I did not know, though I would
come to understand and fear evil,

that, likewise, goodness and mercy
would follow me all the days of my life.

TAVERN ON THE GREEN

Amid so much "over the top,"
the actual candles in the sconces
are a nice touch. Next to our table,
a couple locked in a showy romance
cannot stop talking. They're anxious
for a deposit in their account tonight.

Little Jimmy Scott sings of love,
Heaven, and the masquerade. He
plants a ghost thistle, purple and gray,
with leaves that gently tangle up
and into the light that left
somewhere ago and far away.
This thistle grows wherever there
is love, destruction, a bargain made.

In accord with Ziryab's sequence,
we finish with a crème brûlée.
In American style, we finish with a cigarette.

DINNER OF GRIEF

Colorful "after five" paper umbrellas
and miniature plastic swords
have not followed us here.

Across the course of tumblers
and baskets of bread, a mirror
on the wall behind reflects

a painting of a figure with pink
roses. Smart and black. Grilled
salmon, onions. Dinner without

pearls. Historic site, catalog
of glories and indignities; bathed,
pleated, sexed. A host of others

have been laid to rest in the west,
their souls delivered by dolphins
to other mysterious worlds.

Losses hammer and burn.
When asked, I oblige,
evoking gardens,

Daniel, Jonah, three
indestructible Hebrew
boys unconsumed by fire;

carefully constructing
each elegy like a building,
as a yet unresurrected body.

Those words... that way.

THE FIELD OF AGINCOURT ON THE DAY OF CRISPIN CRISPIANUS

Shakespeare,
Henry V, IV.vii

Past the watchful fires of the night,
ruminations of the morning's danger,
and the sky thick with arrows and smoke,
your position, Henry, is affirmed
to be in God's hands.

The boys and the luggage lackeys
left protected only by man's
laws of arms:

poor souls — "not a boy left alive"! —
"for whom this hungry war
opens his vasty jaws;"

all those innocent
throats cut.

CORTEGE

This is Texas, the second Saturday
After my brother's death in Florida.
Most October afternoons
Are not so bright and clear as a bell.

The little town we live near
Is full of relatives, independent
In-laws and neighbors; with all the push
And pull of a family, is a family.

Today all the vehicles glut
The road to the cemetery. They
Have come in their dress hats
And boots, wearing their pearls and carrying

Black patent purses. Someone —
To keep it from temporarily turning
Into chaos — has taken up directing
All the shiny pickups and cars.

DINNER AT BAROCCO

The friends I dine with are all doctors.
They talk about *the Junkies* and *the Feds*
and places around the world

we all have been. I wander off
to expel what I've just eaten.
I clean the place as best I can.

A woman reaches for the door
I've just let quietly slip shut.
Hoping I haven't left a trace,

I loiter at the bar, smoke a couple
of cigarettes, and scribble
on the back of an envelope

that someone left behind.
A nearby patron is declaiming
how society constructs itself

out of fear lest the crime of one
of its members bring disgrace
upon the whole community.

The bartender is polite.
Seeing me light up
with a candle, he gives me

a monogrammed book
of matches, which I close
and immediately lose.

VILLAGE IDIOT

I was well acquainted
with my great-grandfather,
and all of his sisters and brothers.

The youngest walked alone
along our small town's street.
His gnarled log fingers

locked behind him.
Humming, hunched over
and always humming;

kind of a throwback
to a God-fearing time.
(Like me, he had been

the baby.) Afraid,
I kept my distance.
Once, by happenstance,

I ventured close enough to actually
hear him. He wasn't growling
words of righteous indignation.

He was murmuring verses
of scripture. Sad heir
trapped in his own soft loop.

LOCAL CODES

I mumble my admiration
for the lamb-shaped stones.

For a moment, it could be spring
and sporadic milkweed parachutes

could be drifting by — but, it is
chillier and each gossamer umbrella

is a white tarantula of snow.
The two with us are younger

and tentative. My mother and I are seasoned.
(We have done this somewhere else before.)

We keep our banter low, keep directing
each other's focus back to the flanking pattern

of trellises and flowers (deduce it has
been taken from his parents' next-door stone).

The fugitive color and condition
of the artificial tributes are showing

signs of weather. New clusters of wild-
flowers clump and curl from her grave.

Though the carved manifest
does not identify her as one of ours,

we groom away a few leaves.
Here, all debts and deceptions

are forgiven. Here, we ask
that mercy not pass any of us by.

CERTAINTY BY DEGREES

for Rand Snyder

An instantaneous burst of recognition
in a glance! What could be you

sitting in a wheelchair,
someone pushing from behind!

The muscles across my chest feel tight,
my collar constrictive. A montage

of city rolls by like one of those jerry-built
vacation Bible school scroll theaters.

Eagerly getting the taxi to swerve
and settle only creates more confusion.

Back beneath the portico's peculiar
lights, I'm winded. You've vanished.

No crescendo, no envoi of zither.

EDGE OF THE KNIFE

de gustibus non est disputandum

Wanted posters / embanked frontier town
the failure of intelligence /
the failure of emergency coordination /
the failure of leadership: Orpheus
hectoring white peonies
as he embarks
through vermilion, fiery turmeric, and ash.

                    *

On some days, vintage views —
of backyard acrobats,
Christmasday cowboys,
Xmas in the barracks — can do it.

On others, photographs
of long-deceased ancestors loiter
at the edge of recollection. But today,
there is no consolation to be had.

Not even a bronze Pan stretched out
piping on the green in campy rest
would entertain (as he once did
in those groves of consternation).

                    *

A familiar trope: the diatribe
of a tortured conscience
full of presumption and little remorse.

The transport of love / the transport
of wrath barely charms you away.

*

The grip of death here
is not the failure of human spirit.

It is more the dangling chain of command.

*

We have called to our god,
"Your rigor adds to our fury!"

One look: faith and doubt:
no match for our despair.

"Fish or cut bait!
No more ordeals."

INDIAN STATUES

They are both tall. Kitsch
a son could love.
Not everybody's cup
of tea.

*

The Tibetans boast of owning statues
that were made during the life of the Buddha.

The legend relates that the first Indian statue
sent to the emperor of China by the king of Magadha
was in recognition of aid lent by the emperor
at a time when Magadha
was attacked by the Yavanas (the Greeks).

This statue was included among the treasures
taken in the mid-seventh century to Tibet
by Wen-Cheng, a relation of T'ang T'ai Tsung
and wife of the Tibetan king Sron 'Tsan Sgam-po.

Perhaps art is about being taken
beyond an unfair and unequal border?

*

I picked up the pair of Thanksgiving Indians
at Job Lot one summer while shopping
with my mother. I remember heartlessly
trawling the aisles, listening
to the heartbeat of her sentences,
mother tongue; Jesus knocking at the door —
his hands and arms opening out

like an Acapulco diver. The shelves
seemed piled with candy corn
and southern ermine. Scalawags!

There among the shelves, we encountered
another younger mother leashing
her equally uninvested son
through the same aisles: boy
with his resentments in check,
boy on the fence.

PART OF THE BARGAIN

Harsh landscape. Harsh chores.
Harsh mingling of the narrows
that gush into the blood cups.

The harshness
promises neither
forgiveness nor relief,

nor does it diminish
the quality of whatever
love is there. In some
cases, enough to bestow
a mysterious namesake.
For some of us, our origins
will seed our ends.

First, home cooking;
and, later, food
as a destination.
Maybe a moor of love.
Being a hungry state,
we eat our way out
into the abundance of the world
and — for as long as we can —
our way back to familiarity...
and, perhaps even more illusive,
to intimacy. We send a picture postcard;
and, later, publish a catalog
of what we have eaten up.
We note how the call of tenderness
or other urgencies beckoned
us to cliques and places
beyond the blood.

Will there be a ceremony?
A shape on water? Will
our name appear in stone?

THE SISTERS OF JESUS

Centuries of portentous, self-righteous
men have not pared us away, will

not pare away our eyes. We continue
to stubbornly gaze out —

even through the translations
and interpretations that go against

the fixed self-possession of our ears:
"and are not his sisters here with us?"

Even without a single record of utterance,
each of our insistent sakes

radiates out
from inside the story

the way the folding flesh
of a contrary hog carcass just after a scald

seems to glow, like
everything that money cannot buy

or a gutted fish
with ruby insides

and a sacred,
burning heart.

FUNERAL SONG

composed for my father's funeral

> "the evening star brings together
> all that dawn has divided"

My brother and I were just like Uncle Henry
and Uncle Jasper. We only knew — at three
and five — that they, like us, had something
to do with white chickens and not having
wives and children. I knew Jasper's cabin
had been up where we went once a year
to pick Indian paintbrushes; that Henry
had lived just across the place in
what had been the old caliche dugout,
over by the foot of Little Mountain.

We went once a year over to mow and rake
the cemetery. Our grandparents didn't like
one bit that burrs and Johnsongrass
grew there. Unable yet to read, we
watched for lonely lizards; traced letters
with our fingers; helped pull up goatheads;
gave our favorite stones a kiss. Angels.
Shells. One kneeling marble lamb. We worked
the puzzle, but couldn't make the pieces fit.

Our grandmother explained about how we loved
God because he first loved us. That he came down
to us as a dove. And, when we died, that we
would all become doves and fly away together.
My grandma knew everything. She had already
helped us out with Santa Claus and clouds.

A week later, a family friend who lived
in a city came for a visit. Late in the afternoon,
by the sound of his real gun popping in the distance,
we knew he was up at the tank. That's where
we watched the doves come in the evening
to water. By the time he drove up, it was nearly
dusk. My father carried us out to see him.
With my bare toe I could feel the metal grommet
of Poppa's blue jean pocket. They talked.
But over in the bed of the truck, on streaked
cardboard, lay a pile of bloody doves.

*

One holds the casing.
Someone else's hand
outlined against the blue
brings the lid down.
No real persuasion
to align the parts.
Wrists wobble,
ripple
        (mismatched),
crooked on the groove.

Departure flutters,
        collapses
like a drop on impact:
a single, downward,
empty-of-conviction
thud. Exhausted, all
fervor rubbed out.

Tiny gestures rise
into rings, escalate;
until someone else's
throat lets the dove
out a third time.

BUT AT THE CHURCH

I didn't mind that someone
had seen fit to drape his coffin
at the funeral home or graveside
service. Who can deny "Taps"
its force? I understood

there were many grieving
who saw him as a patriot
who had survived
and returned to thrive
in peace for another sixty years.
And I — oddly sharpened by grief —
appreciated their veteran
loyalty and desire to bid him
a fraternal farewell. But

we were not a military family.
Hadn't he really just been a kid
trying to stay alive; and much
of that time probably not very sober?

The "war years" had preceded us...
me. And I had my misgivings
about any cohort
possessing a force
some of us feel best left
only in the hands of God.

THESE SISTERS

for E.F.

We hope our deaths will find us
in a large quiet room; the modest eyes
of an obedient pet, friends, or ancestry
nearby; an opened book or window,

a song like an arrow, a breeze. This
long day feels as if it will never end:
the uneasy hour, the plangent call,
the ludicrous narrative of a loved one's

last hour in the belly of the beast:
tubes, scissors, and the well-intended
web of science and the clinical arts,
the vain and noble Keystone Kops.

Tonight, our agitated city's sublime.
The embrace of a friendship or a midnight
caller is simply a telephone away.
Highwaymen work the subways.

Before taking stock or lighting a candle
for the death of one of my friend's sisters,
allow all those who didn't know her
time to ask, "What was her name?"

FOOTNOTE IN THE CATALOG OF WEAPONS

*The Sirens have a still more fatal weapon than their song
. . . someone might possibly have escaped from their
singing; but from their silence certainly never.*

Kafka

The daughters of Terpsichore
by the river god Achelous
        lived in a meadow
filled with the bones of men who perished,
            men drawn to their rocks by
        the irresistible
            lure of their song.

        The Argonauts — who
        found on board the song
        of Orpheus sweeter than theirs —
passed by unharmed.
            Their passing was not,
        however, without event.
Young, beloved Butes leapt overboard.
        Aphrodite had to snatch him
        from the waves. O Aphrodite,
watch our astronauts.

        Later, Circe warned Odysseus
about their voices, that he would
        have to pilot his ship
        past their treachery.

            When he did,
            two of them, winged,
        fell to their deaths
        (a celebrated vase painting);

because he, tied to a mast, ears stuffed with wax,
        resisted their song.

A manifold association:
      death and winged creatures, the soul
      and the body, the soul leaving the profane
body in the form of a bird.

        What resides (the question inevitable
in any aftermath)
        in the nature of the Sirens?
        Sound and silence, body and spirit,
          escape and inescape?

AT UNIVERSAL GRILL

for T.A.R.

I slopped hogs. You shoveled shit.
But neither of us walked
five miles to school in the snow.
As the story goes, our fathers did.
While you have built, installed
rainwater cisterns, added on
a traditional porch overlooking
the central Texas hills,
I have become the other mouse.

On the wall behind the bar, four
colorful tambourines hang from nails:
red, white, green, blue. We shift
from old friends we have lost track of
to old friends lost. The aperture
kicks open and an angel passes.

The theme music to television's
I Dream of Jeannie inescapably flutters
above the dining room like a bird in the house.

Our waitress and three waiters wearing
colorful construction-paper bonnets
prance out carrying a plate of something
topped off with a flickering candle.
They surround the table next
to ours. They festively tamp
and shake tambourines in unison.
This third night of your visit
is someone else's birthday.

THE LAST CHILD

First my older brother;
and then my sister, the eldest:
                        our sense of order
so disrupted. The doctors
and empathetic hospice workers
                did their best
with procedures, medicine,
                and instruction. My parents,
humiliated, tired, and aging —
themselves declining — did their best.

                                Years

later, serving as a juror,
        I couldn't help
                but sift through
the motes over the bar of justice.
        How clear!
Ultimately, no drama
of an august body
decides rectitude. The law
rules not because it is right.
        It is FINAL
                as somewhere
                something
                or someone
has to stop —
        had to stop —
                the cycling
                vengeance.

MESSAGING

Shakespeare's travel-weary and timing-savvy
messengers commentate with care
(... *expert riders. Orphans preferred:*
receiver beware)

all the news that's fit... to deconstruct...
news... with which to be in performance,
mysterious winding medium of offer

with which to try and waver
the audience's obstinate gaze.

Literally, from one's tongue
to the actual ear of whoever
has to pay the price — a soulful
Antony alone with an armed Fred;
a quixotic Cleopatra, her Ethels near;

what we'll do to your walled city
if you don't surrender.

This year, my slightly grotesque
homemade valentine equivocates, *Be mine;*
reads: "Viv and me / plus / Tom and you.

Hurry up, please. It's time."

ROSE HILL

Beyond the top limit of the limbs of ancient
Rose Hill elms, a bank tower clock
and a horizon line floating into the late afternoon
evoke the dyed gloaming of a '30s postcard;
a faint copper wash melts
into an arch of more substantial blue.
The tops of the trees are spindly and exuberant.
Lots of breakage means a profusion. A ballet
of limbs crosshatches the view.
                          This April,
before the season of leaves, the trees' newest
tendrils are all comedians dropping little green
tufted chandeliers. In late afternoon, leaf
edges — thin as paper — take their harmonic
peridot from the sun. In all of the elegant
mayhem hovers one of my late, witty brother's
spontaneous performances of Chekhov's
promise of *Moscow in the Spring*.

RESTRAINT

. . . and you do not need to expect
you can rise beyond suffering.
Marie Ponsot, "Reading a Large Serving Dish"

I've seen the ugly, raised heads
of Rivalry, Malice, and Subdued Hunger.
Balance is a justice not so easily
maintained in our present separation

of domain. There is always
an audacious kernel of truth,
though some versions get a lot wrong.
Many inevitably opt for melodrama

colored in with glamour. I ate
six pomegranate seeds. You were
a fierce table host, but there were
no leashes. Mild potions and portions,

and an inevitable seduction.
The anxieties of some storytellers
portray my self-possession more
reduced than it actually ever was.

Now — in geographies I never
dreamt of — God-fearing gardeners
whisper my name as they teach scores
of children to graft fruit trees.

Maps, clippings, and botanical exhibits
wait for me on tenterhooks. Each
year, in the middle of March, my mother,
full of anticipation, still sleeps in her shoes.

DON'T CLING TO ME

Each pair of shoes left
to be attended by the living

is for a moment holy.
The wing tips, the favored high heels

or sandals, each pair
of Byzantine imperial reds

recapitulate the one among the many,
one's emanating jewel-studded halo —

maybe it alternates rubies and pearls —
one courtier emitting among the multitude.

Each allotted heart pumps
whatever opportunity or wisdom

happens to be flowering. None
are divinely winged, cyclical,

or mythic. Each is but a separate
lot robed in a colorful

in-and-out-of linearity;
each, but a singular coil

hosting its own unique
moment of the dance.

"Do not cling to me."

SPRING WINDOWS

at ABC Carpet, 2003

From across the street, a brilliant swirl
of blue, pink, and orange retracts in the back
like a genie's cloud in the window of a diorama:
abstraction of a colorful sky at sunset.
Literally, a drape. Actually, a flock,
a plethora of small artificial birds.
In the next window, they coagulate
into an "afghan" falling over
and down a real chair. In yet the next,
a colorful spiral of butterflies coils up
from a decorative chandelier resting
on the floor. In still another, a clothesline
is pinned full of elegantly striped dish towels.
The clothesline — colorfully edged
in a matching line of the little feathered
creatures — stretches over a hammock
piled with brightly fringed pillows.
No. The little dickenses edge the top
of every pillow too! Hitchcock! Mad
display designer's fabulous use of
insistency! There is always another text.

AMERICAN NIGHTS:
IN MÉRIDA, THE YUCATÁN

Calle 62, five eleven, one block
from the zocalo, we found Sevilla,
already reminiscent of points
east (Andalusia, Chaouen), one great,
weathered wooden door, a dusty,
modest sign — no rating forks or stars,
faint letters shedding little light,
and most of its last layer of exhausted
ancestral paint. Nothing outside —
or in the lobby, for that matter —
hinted of the arched colonnade,
of marble lions standing guard
like a pair of temple dogs, each fiercely
turning in toward the stairs, each
rolling a globe beneath one of his feet.

On the walls, carefully patterned *azulejos*.
On the floor, alternating diamonds
checking up to our room, itself right off
the upstairs colonnade. Everything
as demure, clean, and tended as the stars;
not the least, the potted courtyard plants.

We spoke of Uxmal, Kabah, Sayil,
Labná, and Jean Laffite; of flamingos
and bubbling springs. That night,
among the other mysterious,
almost irresistible Mayan sites,
both the windowed temple
and the dark foot-shaped depths
of Xlacah — the well we would
not see at Dzibilchaltún —
quivered in our sleep.

INDIAN SUMMERS

More than lush. Loaded. Like a stick of dynamite
with a slow, lit fuse: maybe a tearing candle
on a keg of gunpowder. . . in a ship. . .
like the one that alchemistically shuttled
slaves, molasses, and rum to gold. In time,
even starched barbarity, epically attempting
to contort new subjects into a singing serfdom,
resigned. The *encomenderos* failed to convert
themselves to a feudal Mediterranean *latifundio*
sanctified by a Spanish crown. Now, the land
has another border and the dreams of two
postcolonial states. On some level, our peace,
like the smoking tomahawk, has been engineered.

In the real summer in Texas, bats up from Mexico
still devour mosquitoes; actual houses have been
maintained for them by wise and appreciative
stewards of the land. "Bat houses?" some
of the intrepid but perplexed strangers ask.
Traveling in New England, "Indian summers. . .,"
I remember thinking: "Strange terrain
of adjectives and nouns: strange successions
of wills and scattered rationales."

ALL DRESSED UP

"Industrious, honest, frugal...
but never miserly." It was said
of Sarah Wilson, the first
woman in America to endow a college for women,
that she enriched herself reading
by "a lamp of fat." Today,
from over the mantel,
her countenance gazes down —
electrically lit by brass chandeliers.
One can study her face — framed
in a modest bonnet —
in the Wilson College cafeteria.
Doubtful that she could foresee girls everywhere
and kitchen boys — sultry young cutie patooties —
dutifully scraping uneaten food off plates.

It's barely a cross-stitch from Lincoln Tunnel
to the fall mists of Pennsylvania's Blue Mountain.

Danny Elfman's theme for *Edward Scissorhands*
accompanies us through the shadowy gray
wind; over the appaloosa copses
of pollen mustard, tawny orange,
and the sheared kelly meadows.
There is an occasional blush
of mangosteen red, a moist black fence,
ponies, a football stadium,
the highest point of trees
dandelioning out:
a negative burst
of cold fireworks
fretting on the dull
early gray of evening.

"God hates sin, homosexuality, abortion"...
and something else. Kind of a modern
Burma-Shave. Clearly philosophy
has a long tradition in these hills.
Likewise, palomino cornfields have long
marked the October way to Norland Hall,
Alexander McClure's residence
in Chambersburg, Pa.

In the summer, thirsty horses
still arch and slake
at the banks of the Con.

But fall is a different set of Crayolas.
The silhouettes of trees scissor
into the moisture-dulled metal dusk.
Cushionless lawn-divan frames
and barn chakras and windows
fade beside the houses' kitchens
and dining rooms lighting up.

In Norland Hall, in one bedroom,
stately and Victorian, one can find
a pair of extraordinary lamps.
The lovely ample room
is a perpetual impediment
to the union of the pair —
a matching pair of Venetians
that Lord Byron would have
loved. A pair of European gentry
dressed up in Ottoman turbans,
puffy pants, and curl-toed shoes.

The precision of his mustache curls
over the slick of his porcelain cheek.

Her distinct finger and thumb
pinch a flower with the same cultivated
delicacy a Dresden tongue employs
pronouncing the antepenultimate
syllables of "*Ma*honey" or "Iphe*ge*nia."

CHARLES LAUGHTON

*. . . while on top. . .were specimen vases, filled with
spring blossoms and single branches of foliage, which
they had brought back from the country and arranged
with exquisite taste.*

John Gielgud

I never saw you live on stage.
It would have been a pleasure
to have had you for tea and *brazo*
gitano; to have spoken with you

regarding *The Private Life of Henry VIII*'s
images of food, music, and sex;

or of how you had Henry — just after that scene
of the three executioners donning their masks —
study himself while sitting in a bright window seat
(Thomas Culpeper holding the small square mirror).

Later, you had the sovereign stand
alone before one of the stark walls
atop a white corridor of stairs;
had him primp in a small round mirror
drawn from one of his cumulous royal sleeves.

In another scene, at table, he spoke
about the decline of manners;
never missed a beat while his teeth
greedily relished and degloved chicken legs
and his oily fingers haphazardly dispatched
the worthless bones over his shoulders.

Besides the unrequited springs of Bligh
and Quasimodo, I would like
to have spoken with you most
about Captain Kidd and his sartorial
valet's, "Pity about the hair...
I suppose you've tried everything";

or of Shadwell walking in on
his master squirming with ambition
before a mirror hanging in his cabin.

On his own, Captain Kidd must have
toddled to that gaudy Chekhovian sash,
sad flag of hope, the one you paraded
about his girth in the movie's final scene.

I would like to have asked you questions
about: the bowl of American roses
on Effie and Egbert's table;
Prunella Judson's goldfish and meat sauce;

Lincoln at the Silver Dollar; Nell Kenner's
Red Gap beer bust, "ditto boom," cradle of love;

the lovely collage Brecht made for you;
one of the paintings in your collection,
Horace Pippin's *Cabin in the Cotton;*

about Kipling, Robert Mitchum,
Agnes Moorehead, Marilyn;

King Lear;

about verisimilitude, dimensionality, aimlessness, ascent;

about the transforming power of subtext and respect.

PORTRAIT OF HARTLEY

Marsden Hartley, George Platt Lynes, 1943

It is a little like being in a city
and taking a victoria, romantic
by our notions of transportation,
downtown to the site of ancient ruins.

This is not Berlin of 1913 or 1922;
not the promise and resilient
self-worth of a boasting cosmopolitan,
no rings or flamboyant perfumes.

No Rothko-shaped cloud hovers here
in a summer sky behind a red curtain.
No Demuth curve. A shadowy,
engulfed young man, votive and totemic,

leans not far away. Madawaskan
athlete; Canuck Yankee lumberjack;
some beloved drawn up
from a pool of mourning?

Once, of your paintings, a critic wrote —
with beauty and cruelty curling
in his words: "a cold ferocious
sensuality seeks to satisfy itself."

Another day, another catalog:
a seasoned eye, the epic simplicity
of a discriminating dandy's
mature taste, poor circulation,

and — these are not the banks
of the Androscoggin, 1910,
or the beach of Cannes, 1925 —
a three-buttoned, uncuffed suit.

NUREYEV'S FEET

for Arlyn García-Pérez

My friend's loops have always served up treasures;
Rarely a trawler of her own Sargasso Sea.
While wrenching Band-Aids, she mumbles
Something about preventing calluses.
Something she had learned... I lean in a little;
And, sure enough, there it is: the center
Of her story, a marrow, glistening and succulent,
Nureyev's feet.
                    It seems she, front center,
Had a great view of them at a performance
Of *The King and I.* Unexpectedly,
She could see for herself how the great
Artist had pressed them for everything.

PRACTICE FITTING: MARIE PONSOT

for E.F.

Back then, she loved us because we were
young and eager (we stammered full of wonder),
not because we were right. More than once,
she referred to us as young wobbly birds
airing our feathers, warbling our untested
best. You read us a draft of meeting
some phantom of yourself on the stairs.
I thought for a moment — rather than down
to a glass, sunlit vestibule, door, or street —
                that you had us
                  dropping
        into some uncharted
           primal darkness.
I envisioned macabre laughter,
    a gallows door
        dropping;
considered how darkness
        often appears
            to accompany
    the revelation
      of an underlying
        reality.

Later, as we chirped and rode together down
the building's stately elevator, she reached out
and stroked the lovely rich wooden walls.
It was a spontaneous gesture of inspection,
full of reverie; vaguely familiar —
of painters' subjects portrayed
before mirrors. Only here, the catalyst
for reflection was not a mirror.

BUSINESS REPLY MAIL

FIRST-CLASS MAIL   PERMIT NO. 43   PORT TOWNSEND WA

POSTAGE WILL BE PAID BY ADDRESSEE

Copper Canyon Press
PO Box 271
Port Townsend, WA 98368-9931

So, what do you think?

Book Title:

Comments:

Can we quote you on that? ☐ yes ☐ no

Copper Canyon Press seeks to build the awareness of, appreciation of, and audience for a wide range of emerging and established American poets, as well as poetry in translation from many of the world's cultures, classical and contemporary. To receive our catalog, send us this postage-paid card or email your contact information to poetry@coppercanyonpress.org

NAME:

ADDRESS:

CITY:

STATE: ZIP:

EMAIL:

☐ Send me *Editor's Choice*, a bimonthly email of poems from forthcoming titles.

COPPER CANYON PRESS

www.coppercanyonpress.org

The gesture was childlike, free
from any anxiety of display: the self
contemplating the limit of its own estate.

She mentioned how — when she was a girl —
the elevator walls, beneath their luster,
were all rich and somber; how each ride
made her feel as if it were a practice
final fitting. Her devoted daughter —
rolling her eyes to the cubic air —
said, "What a *morbid* thought!"

You and I were entertaining how
we loved her — one of our great
poetry teachers — not because once
she had been young, but because
she was private, curious, and right.

BLUE SEVILLE

Enough of that old invincible sapper, Thirst,
Relentlessly undermining the unheld
Spell of Sleep! It is an hour such as this
That one could almost

Succumb to Breton's proclamation:
The simplest surrealist act consists of going
Out into the street, revolver in hand,
And firing at random

Into the crowd as often as possible.
In the mirror of the miserable armoire,
Where there might once have stood a modest boy,
My salty torso

Hovers like a dimly lit chandelier. My
Humorless twin drinks beside the orange sink:
A sultry friar, sheened in tangerine,
With a glass up

To his lips, a glowing beard of bronze moss,
And a shameless hard-on in the almost
Aimless blades of light. The inevitable
Bright morning,

Patient vanquisher, stands just outside the panes
And mullions, has installed itself outside
The unusually high, heavily curtained windows
Above the bed.

The planes here, including those in the mirror,
Are as complex as a Velázquez interior.
In one, you lie across the bed, gathering
Its electric

Blue counterpane into your downturned face,
Sprawled — I think — like an unprotected corpse.
Once there might have been a romantic coupling.
Once there might have been

A trellis of pink, or a field of turquoise.
But the bells this morning already seem to know
Where we are, how I want to take you, that I burn
To split you at the heart.

BLOOD PRESSURE

We were offered the old extremes of being
either burned to bitterness or refined to gold.

We stayed in town for only one season —
the one marked by Kennedy's assassination
and funeral. Late some of those nights,
the voices and discords of next-door sons,
drunk and disrespectful of *their* mother,
interrupted the spell of the somber telecasts.

I recall only one eruption of *my* mother's
violence. Once — I've always suspected
it deeply rooted in the neighbors' flashes
of profanity that previous season —
she clobbered my cocky teenage
brother on the side of the head
with the wand of a vacuum cleaner.
Her strike, defensive and spontaneous,
curbed any direction toward adolescent
disrespect, and scared us all.

One Sunday morning later that same fall,
I was perplexed to find my mother stifling
tears at the after-church porch-gathering,
the Methodists and Church of Christ neighbors
a stone's throw across the street.
Later, heading back home, she tried
to explain to my sister, brother, and me
about the three little girls shivering
in familiar summer-weight charity.

In her own way, she was coding
and decoding mysterious empathy.
We all knew she knew about
that instant of risking the line
between discipline and damage.

FILICIDE

You, on a tirade, howl
and clang through the vineyard.
Every day the world used to reveal
itself in an orthodoxy: every station
a clear costume; mindfulness
being the one desirable abiding place
for mystery: passion, abyss,
fire to get across. Come back,
sweet clarity, sweet cleansing
fire, one's previous world
of clear and determinable forms.

Jason, the modern sacker,
won't be coming dressed
in a pirate outfit — sporting
a cockade or styling
fashionable leggings.

You can come through
the world's catalog
of great faiths: love
in obedience, submission, action. . .

but you will never return
to the country of your birth.

You will reach the end
of your road a concealing
foreigner, a contrarian,
adrift in oblivion; love
in disobedience;
resistant, inconstant,
and defying translation.

You, destroyer of chattel,
great heroine, will end
— no going back —
in the world's catalog of
self-possessed criminals: murderer
of your brother; in the ledger
of great assertions: will
behind the proprietary
murder of your own children.

    *

The familiar landscape drains me pale,
maintains our winding entourage of grief.
Once, when I was a modest boy unaware
of the river's intractable ordinariness,
a woman — vaguely familiar, like one
of the characters in an ancient play —
came and asked permission to leave the road.
She wanted to go down to wash her hands
in the river. "Sovereignty of mind," mumbled
one of the old women who watched and knew.

    *

It is not that one simply lays down
one's or another's life;

what defines genuine sacrifice
separate from wanton slaughter or squander
is the state of the hand that holds the knife.

BY THE CHARLES RIVER

So much for all those Edwardian allusions:
Down by the washing shallows, the trembling virgin
Stroking the fork of the tree, or *swans' necks*
Crossing. Here, the darkness quietly devouring
The light splintering on the water is simply
The focus of the eaten's hunger. A reminder
To button back up the spiritual and tuck away
The physical until the next bout. The green

Always vowing to the frowning image
Of a disagreeable god, "Forgive me this once.
I will never do this again." The clearer
Who have fought on to the principles behind
Their notions leave savoring some form of,
"Death is the trigger that makes us eternal."

OTHER VISITORS

In the meantime, I've entertained
other visitors; the specters of ancients:
Sappho, Theocritus, Apollonius. . .

all quite smart about art.
Seeking the familiar,
they ask to see, huddle over,

and admire contemporary
poems. During one visit,
the word "psychedelic"

perplexed; created quite
a titter; and, finally, a hum.
Each has demonstrated an interest

in our honey, soaps, and animals.
One, referring to a hippo,
mumbled, "River horse."

Occasionally, I've entertained
them with a crisp cold apple;
a branch of frozen grapes;

a glass of chilled wine.
Oddly, not one of them
has ever expressed perplexity

or an interest
in any of our mechanical
technologies. I am left

considering the relative
depth of our humanity
and the shelf life

of the glamour cast
by the engineered
components of our world.

BRUEGEL'S *PROCESSION TO CALVARY,*
1564

At first glance, this is a stretch
of people filling
a countryside. All appear
to be European; most are men.
There are lots of clothes: tall boots,
tights, bright overshirts,
caps and dark capes. A man,
recognizable as some kind of
soldier by his brick red shirt,
dots across the canvas.
At its center, he sits,
uniformed, astride a horse. Below him
is a man beneath a cross.
Like a Victorian
pop-up card that folds down
in segments, the scene fans out and around
in an inclined uphill swirl.
The procession seems
to have swirled out from a city
located between those distant buildings
on those distant blue ridges
and that less distant,
grandly gated, Flanders-yellow wall.

It is a cold crisp day in early spring;
the ground winks patches of brightly
lit green. The small figures
cast tiny trudging shadows.

At its creaking heart, the clopping procession
has just left the brioche-colored
road. The red horse
and the front wheels of the tumbrel

just now dip into a narrow, shallow draw
of water the pale color
of a dull brocade.
Two children lark across it
on stepping-stones that look to me like
yellow loaves of bread strewn
in the mucky seep.
The seep is a minor inconvenience,
a single episode.
A more significant
commotion takes place back in
the just-broken column.
A local is being solicited
to help carry the other's cross. His
wife tries desperately to hold
him back. A man in red
and white striped tights has raised
his spear to her supplications.
All of this
moves across to that peculiar,
coalescing,
dark ring in the top corner
of the painting. The center of the circle
is green. The crosses for the two
men in the tumbrel have
been erected already. Up here,
it is but a little leap of the eye up
to that magpie perched — no... that *crow*
perched against that cloudy,
intense blue part of the sky.
Here the tree is pole and where once there were
limbs, there now are only spokes.
There is a rag of cloth,
no doubt remaining from the last
wheeled soul. The enclosed circle here is blue.

INTERIOR WITH AN EGYPTIAN CURTAIN

Henri Matisse, oil on canvas, 1948

The bold pattern of an African curtain near us
edges the scene. Four rectangles frame

the radiant flecking of a date palm.
In a couple of panes, touches of blue

hint at a bright clear sky. Short green
and black intervals zipper sweeps of yellow.

The exultant corona of fronds radiates
from where the window's thin black muntins

cross. Just beneath the window, a shallow
dish of fruit casts a scrupling shadow.

Dish and shadow, combined, divides
a floating pink into two corresponding

fragments of ground. Here, since 1948,
a long, thin patch of mellow smears

has bound together everything —
curtain, window, and world.

NOTES TO POEMS

"AIDA"

Gebel Barkal was the original coronation city in the Nubian kingdom of Cush. The anomaly at the bend in the Nile was revered as the residence of Amun Kamutef in all his forms (and thus was the source of the royal *ka*, or soul, which made the pharaoh divine).

UNDEPENDABLE

"If he is so weak, then smash in his head with a rock."

"I bring meat. Everyone doing okay?
You've been working very hard and my father
is very pleased with . . . the fence."

SCANDAL FATIGUE

And luxury lies not in richness and ornateness but in the absence of vulgarity.
Coco Chanel

GOODS

> *Those whose actions are guided*
> *by love, live forever. Love*
> *is the bond between men,*
> *the way to teach,*
> *and the center of the world.*

FALLING MAN

Beckmann, 1950, as recorded to have interpreted one of his canvases to his wife, Quappi.

TAVERN ON THE GREEN

Abdul-Hasan Alí Ibn Nafi (c. 789–857), known as Ziryab, was the aesthetic teacher of the Andalusian court under the amir Abd ar-Rahman II of the Umayyad Dynasty. Among other things, he is credited with being the first to lay out the sequence of courses from salad to postprandial sweets.

EDGE OF THE KNIFE

Don't argue about taste.

THE SISTERS OF JESUS

and are not his sisters here with us?: Mark 6:3.

ALL DRESSED UP

Conocheague Creek in Pennsylvania.

ABOUT THE AUTHOR

Scott Hightower, a native of Texas, is the author of two earlier books of poems, *Tin Can Tourist* (2001) and *Natural Trouble* (2003). He frequently travels in Spain, Morocco, Italy, and Mexico; and he lives in Manhattan where he enjoys collecting vernacular photographs (vintage snapshots). He is a contributing editor of *The Journal* and *Barrow Street,* and a teacher of writing at New York University/the Gallatin School.

The Chinese character for poetry is made up of two parts: "word" and "temple." It also serves as pressmark for Copper Canyon Press.

Founded in 1972, Copper Canyon Press remains dedicated to publishing poetry exclusively, from Nobel laureates to new and emerging authors. The Press thrives with the generous patronage of readers, writers, book-sellers, librarians, teachers, students, and funders — everyone who shares the conviction that poetry invigorates the language and sharpens our appreciation of the world.

Major funding has been provided by:

The Paul G. Allen Family Foundation
Lannan Foundation
National Endowment for the Arts
Washington State Arts Commission

For information and catalogs:

COPPER CANYON PRESS
Post Office Box 271
Port Townsend, Washington 98368
360-385-4925
www.coppercanyonpress.org